Shaken, Not Stirred. A Vodka Lover's Guide to Martinis & Bloody Marys

Featuring 101 of The Best Vodka Cocktail Recipes

Matthew Papcun

First Printing, 2012

Printed in the United States of America

Dedication

To all of those with whom I've shared a drink along the way
and my loving and supportive family and girlfriend, *salute.*

Table of Contents

INTRODUCTION

Vodka is one of the oldest distilled spirits in existence and remains one of the top-selling in the world. Everyone has drank vodka in some shape or form at some point in their life; whether it was in a Cosmopolitan, Apple Martini or one hazy night with a bottle of Popov. Maybe you spent one night on your yacht, rolling around in gold records with a bottle of Ciroc. Ok, maybe that last example was a little reaching but I think we can all agree that it would be awesome.

You're reading this book because you *are* or want to become a vodka drinker. Or maybe you're a long-time bartender, like me, who wants some more knowledge on one of your favorite spirits. Whatever your reason, thank you for taking the time to read my ramblings, and I've got you covered.

As you explore the following pages, you will learn about the history of the most versatile spirit ever made, the differences between grain, potato and fruit-based vodkas and the secrets to making the perfect martini. I also introduce you to vodka's best friend, the Bloody Mary and share with you the history and best recipes of the ultimate breakfast drink.

So read on, my new drinking buddies. Let's get started. But first, I need to refresh my drink.

THE HISTORY OF VODKA

I

Before learning about where it came from, you should know what vodka actually is. Vodka is a distilled spirit. It is comprised mostly of water and ethanol with traces of impurities. It is made with the distillation of grains, potatoes or sometime fruits and sugar (Ciroc was one of the first popular fruit-based vodkas).

Traditional vodka had an alcoholic content of 38% or 76 proof. Today, standard vodkas from Russia and Poland have 40% alcohol by volume (ABV) or 80 proof. The big-wigs at the European Union have established that any "European Vodka" must be 35.7% ABV in order to be called such. American vodkas are traditionally 40% with the exception of some that are 50% ABV or 100 proof.

Eastern European countries and those around the Baltic Sea are known as the Vodka Belt. There, they drink their vodka "neat", meaning there is nothing in the glass except the sweet nectar of water and ethanol. We lightweight Americans usually mix it with juices, soda water, tonic or anything else we can get our hands on because we are babies. I like to add just a *splash* of cranberry juice to mine.

II

What's in a name? Well when it comes to Vodka, a whole hell of a lot. The word "vodka" comes from the Slavic word *voda* which means water and literally translates to *little water*.

The word Vodka first came up in the early 1400's in Poland. Back then, it referred to chemicals such as household cleaners and medicines (yummy). The word used for the actual drink we know and love was *gorzalka* which comes from *gorzec* meaning, "to burn." That seems appropriate to me. "Vodka" was first used to describe an actual beverage in the mid 1500's when referring to a medicinal drink brought from Poland to Russia.

I could write an entire book on all of the different theories about where the word "vodka" came from but I don't want to excite you too much. So, for now, let's just stick with the Slavic translation. It means water and it burns. Deal with it.

III

There isn't much historical material around that documents the origins of Vodka. It's because of this lack of information that there is so much debate on the subject. The biggest argument is that some say it was first distilled in the area of today's Russia in the 9th century and others claim it was Poland that started making it in the 8th century.

As far as the US, vodka became popular in the 1950's and surpassed whiskey as the most consumed spirit in the country by 1975. Which means everyone finally came to their senses. Don't get me wrong, whiskey is great but vodka just makes me feel all warm and fuzzy inside.

A Potato, Grain and Fruit Walk into a Bar...

I

Vodka can be made out of almost anything that is heavy in starch or sugar. The most popular vodkas use either potato or grain. What's the difference you ask? Well, the economy. Vodkas were made from the cheapest thing available at the time. In the middle ages, in Poland, it was grain. The price of grain began to rise so they switched to potatoes.

Some of the most popular vodkas are still made with grain, wheat and rye today. These include; Absolut, Ketel One, Stolichnaya, Belvedere and Crystal Head (filtered through diamonds!).

Potato vodka tends to be much smoother in taste than its grain-based counterpart. Vodkas made with potato include; Chopin, Zodiac, Cirrus, Karlsson's, Chase and Monopolowa.

Ciroc is one the most popular fruit-based vodkas available. It's made from grapes and is great for drinking straight or mixed with juice. Something I've always done with Ciroc that people always get a kick out of is making a shaken, up martini floated with champagne and dropping a frozen red grape in the glass. As the grape thaws, it extenuates the grape flavor of the vodka.

The beginning and the end of the martini end up tasting completely different.

III

I get asked all the time what the best vodka for a martini is. My favorite is one is grain-based from California and its called Hangar One. It is, hands down, the smoothest grain vodka I've tasted. They offer some different flavors as well. What makes their flavored vodka so unique is that they infuse the vodka with natural ingredients rather than using syrups. Infused vodka is simply vodka that is flavored by soaking fruits and/or vegetables in it for a given amount of time, usually two to four weeks.

Infusing Vodka at Home

I'm sure you've been to a bar and seen a giant glass jar filled with pineapples and vodka. That's infused vodka. You can do it yourself at home and on the cheap. All you need is your favorite vodka (Finlandia is great for infusion), some mason jars and a fruit or vegetable of your choice. I'll use my favorite recipe as an example; red jalapeno vodka.

Pick up some Finlandia vodka and about 4 red and green jalapenos from the grocery store. Use a pin to poke holes all over the jalapenos so the oils get released into the vodka. Put the jalapenos in a mason jar, fill said jar with vodka and seal the lid. Let that sit there and think about what it did for about three weeks (a little longer if you want more of a kick). Then strain the vodka into another mason jar or bottle and you are good to go. It's that easy and probably cost you less than two drinks at some fancy-pants bar.

Now that you have your very own fire-vodka, you can use it to make "the most complex cocktail in the world", the Bloody Mary.

SHAKEN, NOT STIRRED

When it comes to martini making there are two questions that you should ask: Do you want it up or on the rocks and with an olive or twist? An "up" martini simply means vodka and vermouth served in a cocktail or martini glass with no ice. Add ice in a highball glass and you've got yourself a martini on the rocks.

A "twist" is usually a twisted lemon peel although it can also be a lime peel. Olives come in all shapes and sizes. They can be stuffed with anchovies, onions, blue cheese or any other food item you can think of.

A common question is, "what's the difference between a 'shaken' and 'stirred' martini?" The purpose of shaking a vodka martini is to make it colder. Shaking is the most common way to mix a vodka martini. The reason James Bond orders his martinis, "shaken, not stirred" is because he wants it cold and he's a pompous ass. The only time you would ever stir a martini is if it were made with gin or whiskey. Stirring a cocktail maintains the "integrity" of the spirit. Gin is a blend of various herbs and spices and shaking it would water it down effectively ruining the intended flavor. Conversely, vodka doesn't have the complexity of gin or whiskey so shaking it doesn't affect it negatively.

One of the biggest mistakes I see people making when preparing a martini is that they think of vermouth as an ingredient. Vermouth is essential to the creation of a martini but it should be used as an enhancement and not an ingredient. To use vermouth properly, pour a small amount in the empty cocktail glass and swirl it around until the glass is completely coated. Then dump the vermouth out of the glass and give it a couple good shakes. Then, pour the shaken vodka into the glass and add a garnish of your choosing. The small amount of vermouth will make the flavors in the vodka "pop" and will make for a much more enjoyable drinking experience.

Now you have all of the information you need to know to sling martinis at your local bar or on your patio with friends. Now let's move on to something that is very near and dear to vodka lovers the world over.

MARY, BLOODY MARY

I

The Bloody Mary is, by far, the most complex cocktail in the world. It can have literally hundreds of different ingredients. Every bartender you ask will have a different recipe they call their own. Mine take about five minutes to make and are definitely worth the wait. I'm not going to go throwing all of my secret recipes out there for the world to see but I will give you one of the best Bloody Mary recipes I've ever seen at the end of this chapter.

II

Like most popular cocktails, the origin of the Bloody Mary is debatable. There are a few different stories as to who created it and where. Fernard Petiot claimed to have created it at the New York Bar in Paris whilst hanging out with Earnest Hemmingway in 1921. Another story is that actor George Jessel created it around 1939 with the recipe of half vodka, half tomato juice.

Fernard Petiot spoke about the drink's creation in The New Yoker Magazine in 1964, seeming to back up Jessel's claim, saying, "I initiated the Bloody Mary of today," he told us. "Jessel said he created it, but it was really nothing but vodka and tomato juice when I took it over. I cover the bottom of the shaker with four large dashes of salt, two dashes of black pepper, two dashes of cayenne pepper, and a layer of Worcestershire sauce; I then add a dash of lemon juice and some cracked ice, put in two ounces of vodka and two ounces of thick tomato juice, shake, strain, and pour. We serve a hundred to a hundred and fifty Bloody Marys a day here in the King Cole Room and in the other restaurants and the banquet rooms."

I find it interesting that Petiot claimed to create the drink in 1921 but later agrees that Jessel came up with the basic recipe in 1939. Either way, it doesn't matter. The drink is still fantastic.

III

The name, Bloody Mary is usually tied to some historical figure; most of the time it's Queen Mary I of England or a fictional woman of folklore. Some "aficionados" believe the name is tied to an actress named Mary Pickford and there is another theory that ties it to a woman named Mary who worked in a Chicago bar called the Bucket of Blood.

IV

The actual recipe for the Bloody Mary is equal parts vodka and tomato juice. However, bartenders around the world have created countless variations to this simple drink. I'm going to list a few of the more popular ones. The first are recipes that replace the vodka with a different form of alcohol.

BLOODY MARY RECIPES

Bloody Beer

Beer, usually a light beer or lager, replacing vodka. Often served with Worcestershire sauce, black pepper, hot sauce, and/or lime.

Bloody Bishop

Sherry in equal measure to vodka

Bloody Cab

Cabernet Sauvignon replacing or in addition to the vodka.

Bloody Fairy, Red Fairy

Absinthe replacing the vodka.

Bloody Geisha, Bloody Ninja

Sake replacing vodka.

Bloody Hogger

Bacon Vodka replacing vodka.

Bloody Jerry

Replace vodka with Madra Rua's Heady Veggie Vodka and add 1 pull (approximately 1/2 ounce) of Guinness

Bloody Maria

Tequila replacing vodka.

Bloody Molly

Irish whiskey replacing vodka.

Bloody Murder

Gin replacing vodka, black vinegar replacing Worcestershire sauce, wasabi sauce replacing horseradish, served with a cherry tomato pierced with a plastic sword stirrer

Bloody Sunshine

Pickle instead of celery, habanero sauce replacing Tabasco. Originated in St. Louis, MO.

Bloody Scotsman

Scotch replacing vodka.

Brown Mary or Whiskey Mary

Whiskey replacing the vodka.

Michelada Clementina (or simply "Chelada")

Mexican beer replacing vodka, usually flavored with a couple of dashes of Worcestershire sauce and Maggi Sauce and Tabasco sauce. Usually made with Clamato (tomato juice with clam juice added). Usually the proportion of beer equals the tomato juice.

Red Eye, Calgary Red Eye, or Saskatchewan Red Eye

Traditionally, beer replacing vodka in a 50/50 mixture with Clamato in place of the tomato juice.

Red Hammer

Through the 1950s in the Northeastern U.S., while vodka was scarce, gin instead of vodka was known as a Bloody Mary; once vodka became readily available in those regions, the traditional vodka-based Bloody Mary was known as a Red Hammer for a time.

Red Snapper, Bloody Margaret or Ruddy Mary

Gin replacing vodka

Virgin Mary, Bloody Shame, Bloody Virgin, or Bloody Barbara

Alcohol free. "Virgin Mary" is commonly used in the USA, and "Bloody Shame" is commonly used in Australia. "Bloody Barbara" refers to Barbara Castle, the British Minister of Transport who introduced tougher drink-driving laws.

V

Next is a list of Bloody Mary recipes that swap out the tomato juice for something else. These are must more common in the bartending community.

Bull Shot

Beef bouillon or beef consommé in place of tomato juice. It may also contain salt, pepper, lemon juice, Tabasco sauce and Worcestershire sauce.

Bloody Caesar

Clamato replaces tomato juice. Much more popular in Canada than the traditional Bloody Mary.

Commander White

Pineapple juice replacing tomato juice.

Bloody Bull

Beef bouillon and tomato juice. The drink originated at Brennan's restaurant in New Orleans and is served at Commander's Palace as well as other Brennan Family Restaurants.

Bloody Eight or Eight Ball

V8 replacing tomato juice, or a mixture, usually equal parts

Bloody Mariyaki

Made with teriyaki sauce instead of Worcestershire sauce.

Bloody Shogun

Same ingredients as a Bloody Mariyaki, but replacing the horseradish with wasabi paste. Created by Jay Buttel and Mike "Double Nipple" Neville.

VI

As promised, here is the best Bloody Mary recipe I have ever tasted. I wish I could take credit for it but it comes from the brilliant mind of Master Mixoligist, Tony Abou-Ganim in his book, The Modern Mixoligist. Turn the page for the recipe for the Blond Mary.

THE BLOND MARY

1 ½ oz chili pepper-infused Finlandia vodka
5 oz fresh yellow tomato juice
½ oz fresh-squeezed lemon juice
Dash balsamic vinegar
2-3 ounces Tabasco green pepper sauce
Pinch ground white peppercorns
Pinch ground cumin
Pinch sea salt
Pinch paprika
Fresh basil sprigs

Add the above ingredients to an ice-filled mixing glass, saving the basil and paprika until last. Roll until blended. Strain into an ice-filled goblet. Garnish with basil sprig and paprika.

Conclusion

There you have it, all of my knowledge on the best distilled spirit around. I hope you have learned something, but, more importantly enjoyed yourself. Please let me know your thoughts in the reviews section on Amazon or on my Facebook page http://www.facebook.com/shakennotstirredvodkaguide and share your thoughts on some of your favorite recipes.

I will be writing more books about other spirits in the near future. Until then, cheers.

101 Vodka Cocktail Recipes

After 14 years of mixing countless drinks, I've forgotten more recipes than are actually on this list. So I reached out to the internet for help with compiling this list. Thank you to everyone who contributed their drinks.

Apple Martini

Ingredients:

2 oz vodka

1 oz green-apple schnapps

Preparation:

Pour the ingredients into a cocktail shaker with ice cubes.

Shake well.

Strain into a chilled cocktail glass.

Black Russian

Ingredients:

1 3/4 oz vodka

3/4 oz coffee liqueur

Preparation:

Build the ingredients in an old-fashioned glass filled with ice.

Stir well.

Campari Cocktail

Ingredients:

1 oz Campari

3/4 oz vodka

1 dash Angostura bitters

lemon twist for garnish

Preparation:

Pour the ingredients into a cocktail shaker filled with ice cubes.

Shake well.

Strain into a chilled cocktail glass.

Garnish with a lemon twist.

Chocolate Martini

Ingredients:

2 oz vodka

1 1/2 oz crème de cacao, white

Hershey Hug or Kiss for garnish

powdered cocoa for rimming

Preparation:

Pour the ingredients into a shaker with ice cubes.

Shake vigorously.

Strain into a chilled cocktail glass rimmed with cocoa.

Cosmopolitan

Ingredients:

1 1/2 oz vodka

1 oz Cointreau

1/2 oz fresh lime juice

1/4 oz cranberry juice

orange peel for garnish

Preparation:

Shake all the ingredients with ice in a cocktail shaker.

Strain into a chilled cocktail glass.

Garnish with an orange peel.

Diamond Martini

Ingredients:

dash of premium dry vermouth

1/2 cup premium grain vodka, frozen

lemon wedge

Preparation:

Chill a cocktail glass.

Pour the dry vermouth and vodka into the glass.

Twist the lemon wedge over the drink.

Run the lemon wedge around the rim of the glass.

Flirtini

Ingredients:

2 pieces fresh pineapple

1/2 oz Cointreau

1/2 oz vodka

1 oz pineapple juice

3 oz Champagne

maraschino cherry for garnish

Preparation:

Muddle the pineapple pieces and Cointreau in the bottom of a mixing glass.

Add the vodka and pineapple juice.

Hairy Navel

Ingredients:

1 oz vodka

1 oz peach schnapps

orange juice to fill

Preparation:

Pour the vodka and peach schnapps into an old-fashioned glass filled with ice cubes.

Top with orange juice.

Stir well.

Long Island Ice Tea

Ingredients:

½ oz triple sec

1/2 oz light rum

1/2 oz gin

1/2 oz vodka

1/2 oz tequila

1 oz sour mix

cola

lemon wedge for garnish

Preparation:

Pour the spirits and sour mix into a collins glass with ice.

Stir well or shake.

Top the glass off with cola.

Garnish with the lemon wedge.

Mudslide

Ingredients:

1 oz vodka

1 oz coffee liqueur

1 oz Irish cream liqueur

Preparation:

Fill an old-fashioned glass with ice.

Pour the ingredients into a cocktail shaker filled with ice.

Shake well.

Strain into the old-fashioned glass.

Sex on The Beach

Ingredients:

1 1/2 oz vodka

3/4 oz peach schnapps

1/2 oz crème de cassis

2 oz orange juice

2 oz cranberry juice

orange slice for garnish

maraschino cherry for garnish

Preparation:

Pour all the ingredients into a cocktail shaker with ice cubes.

Shake well.

Strain into a highball glass.

Garnish with the orange slice and maraschino cherry.

Smith & Wesson

Ingredients:

1 oz vodka

1 oz coffee liqueur

2 oz half and half

club soda to fill

Preparation:

Pour the coffee liqueur, vodka and half and half into a highball glass filled with ice.

Fill with club soda.

Vesper Martini

Ingredients:

3 measures of Gordon's Gin

1 measure of vodka

1/2 measure Kina Lillet

lemon peel for garnish

Preparation:

The Vesper according to Ian Fleming and James Bond:

"Three measures of Gordon's, one of vodka, half a measure of Kina Lillet. Shake it very well until it's ice-cold, then add a large thin slice of lemon peel. Got it?"

-Casino Royale, Chapter 7

Vodka Red bull

Ingredients:

2 oz vodka

Red Bull energy drink

Preparation:

Pour the vodka into a highball glass filled with ice.

Fill with Red Bull.

Admiral Perry

Ingredients:

2 oz Absolut pear vodka

1 oz original cinn schnapps

1 oz dry vermouth

0.25 teaspoon white crème de cacao

thin pear slice for garnish

Preparation:

Add all ingredients to a mixing glass and stir with ice until chilled.

Strain into cocktail glass.

Garnish with a thin slice of pear.

Accomplice

Ingredients:

1 oz simple syrup

2 oz Stolichnaya vodka

1/2 oz fresh lemon juice

Champagne

3 strawberries

superfine sugar for rimming

Preparation:

Muddle three strawberries and simple syrup in a cocktail shaker.

Add the vodka and lemon juice.

Shake well.

Strain into a sugar-rimmed martini glass.

Top with Champagne.

Air Force One

Ingredients:

2 oz Hpnotiq Liqueur

1 oz citrus vodka

juice from a lemon wedge

lemon-lime soda

lemon spiral for garnish

Preparation:

Fill tall glass with all ingredients and add ice.

Stir well.

Garnish with a lemon spiral.

Alabama Slammer

Ingredients:

1/2 oz vodka

1/2 oz Southern Comfort

1/2 oz amaretto

1/2 oz sloe gin

orange juice

Preparation:

Pour the liquors into a highball glass filled with ice.

Fill with orange juice.

Alibi

Ingredients:

1 oz ginger simple syrup (recipe below)

2 oz Stolichnaya vodka

squeeze of a fresh lime

club soda

Preparation:

Pour the ingredients into a cocktail shaker filled with ice.

Shake well.

Strain into an old-fashioned glass filled with ice.

Top with a splash of club soda.

Ginger Simple Syrup:

Peel 2 inches of fresh ginger.

Simmer with 3/4 cup sugar and 1/2 cup water for 5 minutes to infuse flavor.

Remove ginger.

Bottle and chill.

Amarula & Eve

Ingredients:

1 1/2 oz Amarula Cream

1/2 oz Citrus vodka

2 1/2 oz Lychee juice

3/4 oz ruby red Grapefruit juice

Lychee fruit for garnish

Preparation:

Combine all ingredients in a shaker glass filled with ice.

Shake vigorously and strain into a coup glass.

Garnish with lychee fruit on the rim.

Amore Frizzante

Ingredients:

1 oz Van Gogh Vodka

1/2 oz GranGala Triple Orange Liqueur

1/2 oz peach nectar

Prosecco, such as Brunetto

sliced peaches and raspberries for garnish

Preparation:

Pour the vodka, GranGala and peach nectar into a cocktail shaker filled with ice.

Shake well.

Strain into a Champagne flute.

Top with Prosecco.

Garnish with a slice of peach and two raspberries.

Angèle Green Tea Cooler

Ingredients:

2 oz Charbay Green Tea Vodka

2 oz fresh lemon juice

2 oz simple syrup

soda water

lemon wedge for garnish

Preparation:

Pour the vodka, lemon juice and simple syrup into an ice filled highball glass.

Top with soda water.

Pour the contents into a shaker to mix.

Pour back into the glass.

Garnish with the lemon wedge.

Apple Cider Martini

Ingredients:

1 3/4 oz Ultimat Vodka

1 1/2 oz apple cider

1/4 oz ginger liqueur

splash of Velvet Falernum

Preparation:

Combine all ingredients in a shaker.

Shake well and pour into a cocktail glass.

Apple Cin

Ingredients:

1 1/4 oz Van Gogh Wild Apple Vodka

3/4 oz Spiced Rum

1 oz Cranberry Juice

1/2 oz Simple Syrup

cinnamon for garnish

Preparation:

Add Van Gogh Wild Apple Vodka, rum, cranberry juice and simple syrup into a shaker with ice.

Shake and strain into a chilled martini glass.

Garnish with a dash of cinnamon.

Apple Crisp

Ingredients:

1 oz. UV Cake Vodka

1 oz. Revel Stoke Spiced Whisky

1/2 oz. Maple Syrup

2 oz. Apple Juice

Preparation:

Shake all ingredients over ice.

Strain into a martini glass and top with a dash of cinnamon.

Apple Pie Martini

Ingredients:

1 1/2 parts Navan Vanilla Liqueur

1 part Belvedere Vodka

2 parts apple cider

1 tsp cinnamon

squeeze of lime

Preparation:

Pour the ingredients into a cocktail shaker filled with ice.

Shake well.

Strain into a chilled cocktail glass.

April Rain

Ingredients:

2 oz vodka

1/2 oz lime juice

1/2 oz dry vermouth

lime peel for garnish

Preparation:

Pour the ingredients into a cocktail shaker with ice cubes.

Shake well.

Strain into a chilled cocktail glass.

Garnish with the lime peel.

As Night Falls

Ingredients:

2 parts Grey Goose L'Orange Vodka

1 part white grapefruit juice

2 coriander leaves

7 red peppercorns

1 1/2 tsp white sugar

small piece of ginger

whole star anise to garnish

orange zest for garnish

Preparation:

Muddle the peppercorns in a cocktail shaker.

Add thinly sliced ginger and muddle again.

Add the other ingredients and ice.

Shake vigorously.

Double strain into a chilled coupette glass.

Garnish with an orange zest and piece of star anise.

Aspenlicious

Ingredients:

2 parts Pearl Lo Coco (Coconut) Vodka

1/2 part Amaretto

1/2 part Coffee Liqueur

1/2 part rum

1/2 part Irish Crème

splash Half & Half

dash chocolate syrup

topped with grated white chocolate

Preparation:

Coat a martini glass with the dark chocolate syrup.

Wet the rim with chocolate syrup and dip in grated white chocolate.

In a pint glass, mix liquid ingredients with ice, shake and strain into chocolate-coated glass.

Garnish with the grated chocolate on the surface of the cocktail.

Atone-Mint

Ingredients:

2 oz Stoli Blueberi vodka

1/2 oz fresh lemon juice

2 oz sparkling water

1 tsp sugar OR 1 oz simple syrup

fresh mint leaves

lemon wedge for garnish

Preparation:

Muddle the mint and simple syrup in a highball glass.

Fill the glass with ice.

Add the vodka and lemon juice.

Top off with sparkling water.

Garnish with a lemon wedge.

Babel-On the Rocks

Ingredients:

2 parts Kahlua

1 part Stoli Elit

2 parts half & half

Preparation:

Pour the Kahlua and vodka into an old-fashioned glass filled with ice.

Float the half & half on top.

Banana Split Martini

Ingredients:

1 1/2 oz vodka

3/4 oz crème de banana or banana liqueur

3/4 oz crème de cacao

banana slice for garnish

Preparation:

Pour the ingredients into a cocktail shaker filled with ice.

Basil North

Ingredients:

25 ml apple juice

50 ml Cape North Vodka

2 basil leaves

1 freshly squeezed lemon (cut in half)

1 dash of sugar

Preparation:

Pour the ingredients into a cocktail shaker filled with ice.

Shake well.

Fine strain into a chilled cocktail glass.

Beautiful Boat

Ingredients:

40 ml Rose Champagne

50 ml Cape North Vodka

2 mint leaves

Preparation:

Shake the vodka and mint in a cocktail shaker filled with ice.

Double strain into a chilled cocktail glass.

Float Champagne over top.

Berry Whipped (shooter)

Ingredients:

1 oz. Smirnoff® Whipped Cream Flavored Vodka

1/2 oz. Smirnoff® Strawberry Flavored Vodka

Splash grenadine

Preparation:

Mix ingredients in a cocktail shaker and serve in a shot glass.

Berry White

Ingredients:

1/2 oz UV Blue Vodka

1/2 oz crème de cacao

1/2 oz Triple Sec

1/2 oz lime juice

Preparation:

Pour the ingredients into a cocktail shaker with ice.

Shake well.

Strain into a chilled cocktail glass.

Big Breezy

Ingredients:

2 parts Absolut New Orleans vodka

4 chunks fresh watermelon

1 part simple syrup

squeeze of fresh lemon

pinch of black pepper

melon ball for garnish

lemon slice for garnish

Preparation:

Place all ingredients into a cocktail shaker filled with ice.

Shake well.

Strain into a chilled cocktail glass.

Garnish with a melon ball and lemon slice.

Carrot Cake

Ingredients:

1 1/2 oz. UV Cake Vodka

3/4 oz. Carrot Juice

1/2 oz Milk

1/4 tsp. Nutmeg

1/4 tsp. Cinnamon

Splash of Soda

Whipped cream for garnish

Preparation:

Shake first 5 ingredients over ice.

Strain into martini glass.

Celery Cup No. 1

Ingredients:

1 1/2 oz Square One Cucumber Organic Vodka

2" celery stalk (closer to the heart for sweetness)

Palm-full cilantro (1/4 cup)

1oz lemon

3/4 oz agave nectar

1/2 oz Pimm's

1" fresh English cucumber

Preparation:

In a mixing glass, muddle the cucumber, celery, cilantro and lemon juice into a pulp.

Add the Pimm's, agave nectar and vodka.

Cover in ice and shake hard for 10 seconds.

Hawthorne strain tall over fresh ice and garnish with a center piece of celery.

Champanska

Ingredients:

1/2 cup Champagne, chilled

1 oz Smirnoff Black vodka

1 oz lime cordial

lime twist for garnish

Preparation:

In a mixing glass stir together the vodka and lime cordial.

Gently pour the Champagne into a Champagne flute.

Add the vodka and lime mixture to the Champagne.

Garnish with the lime twist.

Cherub's Cup

Ingredients:

1 part St. Germain elderflower liqueur

2 parts vodka, citrus vodka, or Hendricks Gin

3/4 part fresh lemon juice

1/4 shot simple syrup

1 part muddled strawberry

top with Brut Rosé Sparkling Wine

strawberry for garnish

Preparation:

Shake and strain over fresh rocks in a collins glass.

Top with Brut Rose or Brut Champagne.

Garnish with a strawberry.

Chi-Chi

Ingredients:

1/2 cup ice

2 oz vodka

1/2 oz blue curacao

1/2 oz cream of coconut

1/2 cup fresh or canned pineapple

scoop of vanilla ice cream

chunk of pineapple for garnish

Preparation:

Pour all ingredients into a blender.

Blend until smooth.

Pour into a chilled margarita or highball glass.

Garnish with the pineapple.

Christmas Jones

Ingredients:

4 fresh strawberries

1 part vodka

2 tsp superfine sugar

5 oz pineapple juice

7-Up

mint sprigs for garnish

Preparation:

In a blender, whiz the vodka, strawberries, sugar and pineapple juice together.

Pour the mix equally into two highball glasses.

Top with 7-Up.

Garnish with a sprig of mint.

Communitini

Ingredients:

1 1/2 oz Van Gogh Pomegranate Vodka

1 1/2 oz pomegranate juice

3/4 oz lemonade

3/4 oz simple syrup

1/4 oz fresh mint

sugar rim and mint for garnish

Preparation:

Rim a chilled cocktail glass with sugar.

Muddle the mint, simple syrup and lemonade in a cocktail shaker.

Add ice, vodka and juice.

Shake well.

Strain into the prepared glass and garnish with a sprig of mint.

Coriandrum

Ingredients:

2 oz Square One Organic Vodka

1/4 oz Cinzano Bianco Vermouth

splash of coriander nectar (recipe below)

splash of orange bitters

coriander seeds for garnish

lemon twist for garnish

Preparation:

Pour the vodka, vermouth, nectar and bitters into a cocktail shaker filled with ice.

Shake for 30 seconds.

Strain into a chilled cocktail glass.

Garnish with a few coriander seeds and lemon twist.

Coriander Nectar:

Ingredients:

1 cup coriander seeds

4 cup water

1 1/4 cup Madhava Organic agave nectar

Preparation:

Cook coriander seeds and water on very low heat for 30 minutes.

Remove from heat.

Add agave nectar (simple syrup may be used).

Store in refrigerator.

Dark 'n Fluffy

Ingredients:

2 oz. Smirnoff® Marshmallow Flavored Vodka

2 oz. Godiva® Dark Chocolate Liqueur

1 oz. cream

Marshmallows (garnish)

Cocoa powder (garnish)

Preparation:

Mix ingredients in a cocktail shaker and serve in a cocktail glass. Garnish with marshmallow and sprinkle with cocoa powder.

Deep Blue Sea Martini

Ingredients:

2 oz Blue Ice American Vodka

3/4 oz sweet and sour mix

1/2 blue curacao

1/2 oz pineapple juice

Preparation:

Pour the vodka, sour mix, blue curacao and pineapple juice into a cocktail shaker with ice.

Shake well.

Strain into a chilled cocktail glass.

Dirty Bird

Ingredients:

1 oz vodka

1 oz coffee liqueur

cream or milk

Preparation:

Pour the vodka and coffee liqueur in an old-fashioned glass filled with ice.

Fill with milk or cream.

Shake by placing a mixing tin over the glass and giving it one or two good shakes.

Electric Iced Tea

Ingredients:

1/2 oz vodka

1/2 oz light rum

1/2 oz tequila

1/2 oz gin

1/2 oz blue curacao

1 oz sour mix

splash of lemon-lime soda

Preparation:

Build the ingredients in a collins glass.

Stir.

Elit Midnight Millionaire

Ingredients:

1 oz Stoli Elit

Perrier Jouët Fleur de Champagne

raspberry for garnish

Preparation:

Pour the vodka into a Champagne flute.

Fill with Champagne.

Drop a single raspberry in the glass as a garnish.

Espresso Martini

Ingredients:

1 1/2 oz vodka

3/4 oz Kahlua coffee liqueur

1/4 oz white crème de cacao

1 oz cold espresso

Preparation:

Pour the vodka and Kahlua, crème de cacao and espresso into a cocktail shaker with ice.

Shake well.

Strain into a chilled cocktail glass.

Firefly

Ingredients:

2 oz vodka

4 oz grapefruit juice

1 oz grenadine

Preparation:

Pour the vodka and grapefruit juice into a mixing glass with ice.

Stir well.

Strain into a highball glass filled with ice.

Add the grenadine.

Stir again or allow the grenadine to float up from the bottom.

French 76

Ingredients:

1/2 oz lemon juice

1 oz gin

1/2 oz Cointreau

Champagne

Preparation:

Pour the lemon juice or gin and Cointreau into a cocktail shaker with ice cubes.

Shake well.

Strain into a chilled Champagne flute.

Carefully add the Champagne.

Gingerbread Man-tini

Ingredients:

1 1/2 oz citrus vodka

1 1/2 oz Hiram Walker Gingerbread liqueur

1/2 oz dry vermouth

1/4 oz simple syrup

lime wedge for garnish

Preparation:

Rub the lime wedge on the rim of a frozen cocktail glass and leave the lime there for a garnish.

Pour the ingredients into a cocktail shaker filled with ice.

Shake well.

Strain into the glass.

Ginger Sour

Ingredients:

2 oz SKYY Infusions Ginger Vodka

1 oz Lemon Juice

1/2 oz Egg White

1/2 oz Maple Syrup

Lemon twist for garnish

Preparation:

Combine all ingredients in a cocktail shaker with ice.

Shake vigorously and strain into a cocktail glass.

Garnish with twist of lemon.

Godmother

Ingredients:

1 1/2 oz Vodka

1/2 oz Amaretto

Preparation:

Build the ingredients in an old-fashioned glass with ice cubes.

Stir well.

Harrington

Ingredients:

1/8 oz Chartreuse Green

1 oz vodka

1 oz curacao

orange peel for garnish

Preparation:

Pour the ingredients into a cocktail shaker filled with ice.

Shake well.

Strain into a chilled cocktail glass.

Garnish with an orange peel.

Harvey Wallbanger

Ingredients:

3/4 oz vodka

1 1/2 oz orange juice

1/4 oz Galliano

orange slice for garnish

maraschino cherry for garnish

Preparation:

Pour the vodka and orange juice into a collins glass with ice cubes.

Add the Galliano.

Garnish with the orange slice and maraschino cherry.

Hawaiian Iced Tea

Ingredients:

1/2 oz vodka

1/2 oz light rum

1/2 oz tequila

1/2 oz gin

1/2 oz triple sec

1 oz sour mix

1 oz pineapple juice

Preparation:

Build the ingredients in a collins glass.

Stir.

Hello Kitty

Ingredients:

2 parts TY KU liqueur

1 part vodka

fresh lemonade

Preparation:

Pour the ingredients into a cocktail shaker filled with ice.

Shake well.

Strain into a chilled cocktail glass.

Herb's Garden Ale

Ingredients:

2 1/2 parts Herb's Dill Vodka

1/2 part dry vermouth

1/2 part sweet vermouth

Ginger ale

Preparation:

In an empty collins glass, combine vodka, sweet vermouth and dry vermouth.

Add ice.

Top off with ginger ale.

Hollywood Martini

Ingredients:

3 oz vodka

1/2 oz black raspberry liqueur

dash of pineapple juice

Preparation:

Pour the ingredients into a cocktail shaker filled with ice.

Shake well.

Strain into a chilled cocktail glass.

Jolly Rancher

Ingredients:

1 oz Three Olives Green Apple Vodka

1 oz peach schnapps

4 oz cranberry juice

orange wedge for garnish

Preparation:

Pour vodka and schnapps into a highball glass filled with ice and top with cranberry juice.

Garnish with an orange wedge.

Katinka

Ingredients:

1 1/2 oz vodka

1/2 oz apricot brandy

1/2 oz lime juice

fresh sprig of mint for garnish

Preparation:

Pour the ingredients into a mixing glass filled with ice.

Stir well.

Strain into a chilled cocktail glass.

Garnish with a sprig of fresh mint.

Killer Blowfish

Ingredients:

1 oz TY KU liqueur

1 1/2 oz vanilla vodka

5 drops green jalapeno Tabasco sauce

1/2 oz passion fruit puree

1/2 oz fresh sweet and sour

"squirt" of egg white (optional)

Preparation:

Pour the ingredients into a cocktail shaker filled with ice.

Shake well, more if you include the egg.

Strain into a chilled cocktail glass.

Lava Lamp Martini

Ingredients:

2 oz vodka or citrus vodka

1 oz raspberry liqueur

1 oz honey

Preparation:

Pour the vodka into a cocktail shaker with ice.

Shake well.

Strain into a chilled cocktail glass.

Mix the honey and raspberry liqueur well in a shot glass.

Use a spoon to slowly drizzle the honey mixture into the vodka.

LAX Cocktail

Ingredients:

1 1/2 oz Absolut Los Angeles

3/4 oz X-Rated Fusion Liqueur

fresh juice of 1/2 a lime

2 dashes orange bitters

maraschino cherry for garnish

Preparation:

Pour the ingredients into a cocktail shaker with ice.

Shake well.

Strain into a chilled cocktail glass.

Drop a maraschino cherry in the glass for a garnish.

Lovers Lane

Ingredients:

1 1/4 oz Lotus Blue Vodka

1 oz X-Rated Fusion liqueur

1/2 oz lemon cello

1/4 oz fresh lime juice

dash of Angostura aromatic bitters

Preparation:

Pour the ingredients into a cocktail shaker filled with ice.

Shake well.

Strain into a chilled cocktail glass.

Manuka & Maple Sour

Ingredients:

1 part 42 Below Honey Vodka

1/2 part maple syrup

2/3 part lemon juice

dash of bitters

lemon zest and orange peel for garnish

Preparation:

Combine all ingredients in a cocktail shaker filled with ice.

Shake well.

Strain into a chilled martini glass.

Garnish with lemon zest and an orange peel.

Maya Magic

Ingredients:

1 oz Van Gogh Pineapple Vodka

1 oz Van Gogh Vanilla Vodka

1/2 oz triple sec

1/2 oz cranberry juice

pineapple slice for garnish

Preparation:

Pour ingredients into cocktail shaker, and add crushed ice.

Let stand for five seconds, and then shake vigorously for five seconds.

Strain into a martini glass.

Garnish with a pineapple slice.

Natural Selection

Ingredients:

1 oz SKYY Berry vodka

3/4 oz Apple Pucker

3/4 oz Hpnotiq

splash of pineapple juice

Preparation:

Pour the ingredients into a cocktail shaker filled with ice.

Shake well.

Strain into a chilled cocktail glass.

October Screwdriver

Ingredients:

3 oz Blavod vodka

3 oz orange juice

Preparation:

Pour the orange juice into a collins glass filled with ice.

Slowly float the Blavod on top.

Passion Pearl

Ingredients:

1 1/2 oz rum

1 1/2 oz passion fruit vodka

1/2 oz triple sec

1/2 oz lemon juice

2 dashes Angostura aromatic bitters

Preparation:

Pour the ingredients into a cocktail shaker with ice cubes.

Shake well.

Strain into a chilled cocktail glass.

Pink Flamingo

Ingredients:

1 1/2 oz vodka

1 1/2 oz Cointreau

orange juice

dash of sloe gin

Preparation:

Pour the vodka, Cointreau and sloe gin into a highball glass filled with ice.

Top with orange juice.

Stir well.

Polished Princess

Ingredients:

1 1/2 oz. Sobieski Vanilla Vodka

5 cranberries

Pinch pumpkin spice

1/2 oz. fresh lemon juice

3/4 oz. simple syrup

1 egg white

Preparation:

In the bottom of a mixing glass, muddle the cranberries and spice in the simple syrup and lemon juice.

Then add remaining ingredients and dry shake.

Then add ice and shake again.

Strain into chilled martini glass and add 3 floating cranberries for garnish.

Raven

Ingredients:

1 oz vodka

1 oz rum

1 oz blue curacao

1/2 oz Chambord

Preparation:

Pour the vodka, rum and blue curacao into a cocktail shaker filled with ice.

Strain into a highball glass filled with fresh ice.

Slowly pour the Chambord over the back of a bar spoon so it floats on top.

Sinclair's Sunshine

Ingredients:

1 oz Van Gogh Oranje Vodka

1 oz Van Gogh Mango Vodka

1/2 oz triple sec

1/2 oz orange juice

1/2 oz sweet and sour

orange slice for garnish

Preparation:

Pour ingredients into cocktail shaker and add crushed ice.

Let stand for five seconds.

Shake vigorously for five seconds.

Strain into martini glass.

Garnish with an orange slice

Steel Helmet

Ingredients:

1 oz vodka

1 oz coffee liqueur

milk or cream to fill

Galliano liqueur

Preparation:

Build the vodka, coffee liqueur and milk or cream in an old-fashioned glass.

Stir well.

Float Galliano on top by slowly pouring it over the back of a bar spoon.

Tea Tini

Ingredients:

1 3/4 oz vodka

1 oz sweet iced tea

1/4 oz fresh lemon juice

lemon wedge for garnish

Preparation:

Pour the ingredients into a cocktail shaker with ice cubes.

Shake well.

Strain into a chilled cocktail glass rimmed with sugar.

Garnish with the lemon wedge.

Tomojito

Ingredients:

2 oz Three Olives Tomato Vodka

2 lime wedges

cherry tomato

basil-infused simple syrup

soda

lime wedge and cherry tomato for garnish

Preparation:

Muddle 2 lime wedges, 1 cherry tomato and basil-infused simple syrup in a glass.

Add vodka and ice.

Shake well.

Top off with soda.

Garnish with a lime wedge and cherry tomato.

Touchdown Tea

Ingredients:

1/2 part vodka

1/4 part tequila

1/2 part rum

1/2 part gin

1/2 part triple sec

1 1/2 parts lemon-lime Gatorade

splash of cola for color

orange juice for taste (optional)

Preparation:

Fill a punch bowl with ice.

Pour the ingredients into the bowl using the ratios given in the recipe.

Stir well.

Tornado

Ingredients:

1 oz whiskey

1 oz vodka

1 oz rum

1 oz tequila

cola

1 tsp sugar

3 ice cubes

Preparation:

Stir the liquors with ice.

Strain into a collins glass.

Add sugar and stir again.

Add ice then cola.

Stir three times and serve with a straw.

US of A Rocks

Ingredients:

2 oz Skyy Infusions Passion Fruit Vodka

1/2 oz peach schnapps

2 oz orange juice

1 oz freshly squeezed lemon juice

1 oz simple syrup

peach slice for garnish

Preparation:

Shake all ingredients with ice.

Strain into a rocks glass filled with ice.

Garnish with a peach slice.

UV Pink Flamingo

Ingredients:

2 parts UV Lemonade Vodka

1 part cranberry juice

splash of triple sec

Preparation:

Pour the ingredients into a cocktail shaker filled with ice.

Shake well.

Strain into a chilled cocktail glass.

Vampire

Ingredients:

1 1/2 oz vodka

1/2 oz black raspberry liqueur

cranberry juice

Preparation:

Pour the vodka and black raspberry liqueur into a cocktail shaker with ice.

Shake well.

Strain into an old-fashioned glass filled with ice.

Vanilla Vixen

Ingredients:

1 oz SKYY Vanilla vodka

2 oz SKYY Citrus vodka

1 oz Midori melon liqueur

1/2 oz lime juice

Preparation:

Pour the ingredients into a cocktail shaker with ice.

Shake well.

Strain into an old-fashioned glass with ice.

Vodka Collins

Ingredients:

2 oz vodka

sour mix

soda water

orange slice for garnish

maraschino cherry for garnish

Preparation:

Pour the vodka into a collins glass filled with ice.

Fill with sour mix.

Shake by placing a tin over the glass, giving a couple of good shakes.

Add a splash of soda water.

Garnish with a cherry and orange slice flag.

Victoria's Secret

Ingredients:

2 oz crème de fraises

1 oz citrus vodka

1 oz lemon juice

Preparation:

Pour the ingredients into a cocktail shaker filled with ice.

Shake well.

Strain into a chilled cocktail glass with a small amount of ice if desired.

Voodoo Priestess

Ingredients:

1 part Absolut New Orleans vodka

1 part fresh mango puree

1/4 part DeKuyper Anisette Liqueur

1/2 part simple syrup

6-8 fresh mint leaves

Preparation:

Muddle mango puree, mint and simple syrup in an old-fashioned glass for this concoction.

Fill glass with ice and add vodka and DeKuyper Anisette Liqueur.

Stir gently to blend.

Garnish with fresh mint sprig to ward off evil spirits.

Whipped Sunset

Ingredients:

1 1/2 oz. Smirnoff® Whipped Cream Flavored Vodka

3 oz. sour mix

2 oz. pineapple juice

1/2 oz. grenadine

Whipped cream (garnish)

Preparation:

Mix all ingredients, except for grenadine, in a cocktail shaker with ice and serve in a glass.

Top with grenadine.

Garnish with whipped cream.

White Carnation

Ingredients:

2 oz vodka

1/2 oz peach schnapps

2 oz orange juice

soda water

splash of cream

orange slice for garnish

Preparation:

Pour the vodka, schnapps and orange juice into a mixing glass filled with ice.

Stir well.

Strain into a highball glass filled with ice.

Top with soda water and a splash of cream.

Garnish with an orange slice.

White Christmas Dream

Ingredients:

1 oz vodka

1 oz amaretto

1 oz heavy cream

nutmeg for garnish

Preparation:

Pour the ingredients into a cocktail shaker filled with ice.

Shake vigorously.

Strain into a chilled cocktail glass.

Garnish with grated nutmeg on top.

Winter

Ingredients:

1 1/2 oz SKYY Orange vodka

1/2 oz blue curacao

1 oz Champagne

blue maraschino cherry for garnish

Preparation:

Pour the vodka and blue curacao into a mixing glass with ice.

Stir well.

Strain into a Champagne glass.

Top with the Champagne.

Garnish with a blue maraschino cherry.

Widow Maker

Ingredients:

1 part Jägermeister

1 part vodka

1 part coffee liqueur

2 drops grenadine

Preparation:

Combine and shake all ingredients over ice.

Strain into cocktail glass.

Woo Woo

Ingredients:

2 oz vodka

1 Tbsp peach schnapps

1/2 cup cranberry juice

lime wedge

Preparation:

Place the lime wedge into a cocktail shaker with ice cubes.

Add the other ingredients.

Shake well.

Strain into a chilled cocktail glass.

Garnish with a lime wedge.

Yellow Submarine

Ingredients:

1 1/2 oz vodka

1/2 oz white rum

1/2 oz banana liqueur

banana slice for garnish

Preparation:

Pour the ingredients into a cocktail shaker with ice.

Shake well.

Strain into a chilled cocktail glass.

Garnish with the banana slice.

Zen Milk Bath

Ingredients:

1 oz (30 ml) Zen Green Tea Liqueur

1 oz (30 ml) nigori sake

1/4 oz (7 ml) vanilla vodka

2 oz (60 ml) milk

Matcha powder for garnish

Preparation:

Mix all ingredients in a cocktail shaker with ice.

Strain into a chilled martini glass.

Sprinkle matcha powder on top and serve.

Zipperhead

Ingredients:

1 oz vodka

1 oz Chambord

1 oz 7-Up

Preparation:

Build the ingredients in a chilled old-fashioned glass with ice.

Zorbatini

Ingredients:

1 1/2 oz vodka

1/2 oz ouzo

Greek olive for garnish

Preparation:

Pour the vodka and ouzo into a cocktail shaker filled with ice.

Shake well.

Strain into a chilled cocktail glass.

Garnish with a Greek olive.

ABOUT THE AUTHOR

Matthew Papcun grew up in the Detroit area. He began bartending 14 years ago at the age of 18 and is currently the General Manager of Leaf Barley & Vine in Brighton, Michigan.

17959723R00070

Made in the USA
San Bernardino, CA
21 December 2014